ISBN No.978-1-4067-8741-2

THE DECOYING & TRAPPING
OF BIRDS & ANIMALS
WITH NOTES ON LARK MIRRORS

BY
M. BROWNE & J. E. HARTING

EDITED BY TONY READ

TRAPPING

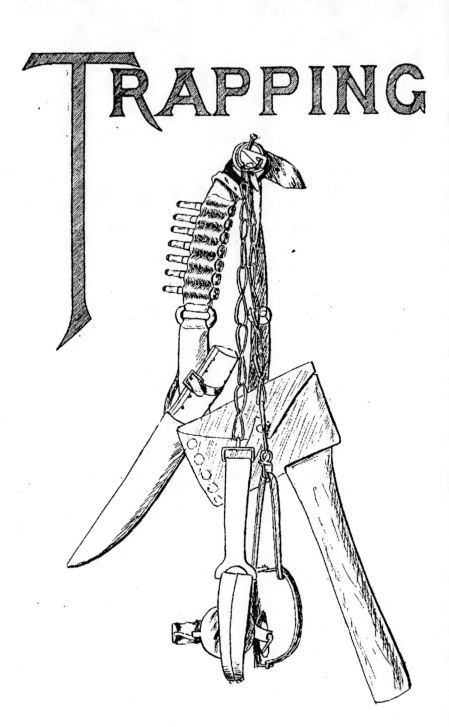

Decoying and Trapping Animals.

THE decoying and trapping of birds, &c., is a somewhat delicate subject to handle, lest we degenerate into giving instruction in amateur poaching; but the application of my direction I must leave to the reader's own sense of fitness of time and scene, and object to be snared. And now, before launching into my subject, one word in season. Observe as a golden rule—never to be broken—this: Do not snare, shoot, nor kill any more birds or animals than you absolutely want—in fine, do not kill for killing's sake, or snare in wantonness. Let all you do have reference to some object to be attained, either to procure specimens wanted for a collection, or, in cases of necessity, for food. Bear this in mind, for, without sympathy with creatures fashioned in as complex and beautiful a manner as ourselves, we can never hope to be true naturalists, or to feel a thrill of exquisite pleasure run through us when a new specimen falls to our prowess. How can we admire its beauty when alive, or feel a mournful satisfaction at its death, if we are constantly killing the same species of bird for sport alone?

Another thing: kill a wounded bird as quickly and humanely as possible, which you may always do by pressing its breast just under the wings with your finger and thumb, bearing the whole weight of the palm of the hand on the sternum or breast-bone, and gradually increasing the pressure until life is extinct. This plan suffices for even the larger birds, provided you can find a means of holding them firmly while you employ both hands in the manner previously indicated.

Again: if collecting eggs, be content with half the sitting

of a nest, and if you know of a very rare nest of eggs, do not take them all in your acquisitive greed. If you see a rare bird, on common land, you may as well secure him as let "Jack Smith" make him up in a sparrow pie; but if the bird is on preserved land, or in a retired spot where no one is likely to harry it, do think a minute before pulling trigger, and ask yourself three questions: 1. Will this bird be likely to stay if unmolested? 2. Is it likely to have a mate? 3. Will it nest here? If you can answer any of these questions in the affirmative, why, "don't shoot, colonel;" for think of the aid to science, and your own satisfaction, if you can discover anything new in its habits, or verify any doubtful point. Many rare birds would nest here if undisturbed, and come again with additions. The Hoopoe, or golden oriole, for instance, and many other rare birds, would nest, and, indeed, do nest here when allowed.

An interesting account of the appearance of the great bustard in Norfolk, and the pains taken through the kindness of Lord Lilford to provide it with a mate, appeared in the *Field* of April 8, 1876. But alas! everyone is not so considerate, and we have but a select few of such self-sacrificing people.

I presume no notice is required how to set the first trap on our list—I mean our boyhood's old favourite, the brick trap, or the sieve and string, both very well in their way in hard weather; but a notice may be required as to the uses to which the next simplest trap, or springe (the horsehair noose), may be applied. For the very few people who do not know how to set it, I will, in the manner of Col. Hawker, who did everything at the time which he wished to explain in writing, proceed to make one. Here, then, I have a black horsehair about two feet long; I double it, holding it between

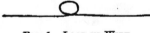

FIG. 1.—LOOP IN WIRE.

the right-hand finger and thumb, leaving a little loose loop of about half an inch long; from this point I proceed by an overhand motion of the thumb to twist it up; on reaching the bottom I make a small knot to prevent its unrolling; then, pushing the knotted end through the eye of the loop, I thus form a loose noose. I then attach a piece of wire to the free end by a twisted loop (see Fig. 1). With about half a dozen of these springes coiled in an oval tin box I am ready to snare any small bird whose haunt I may discover. Birds which are nesting can easily be caught by placing one noose in the nest and others round the edge or mouth, making fast the end wires to any contiguous branch or twigs. Moorhens or water-rails, which swim or run through the constantly frequented tracks which they have made in dense undergrowth or rushes in bogs, may be captured by attaching these nooses to a string stretched across—indeed, a writer in the *Field*, of July 8, 1876, says, speaking of Turkestan :

Ducks are caught by rather a clever arrangement with horsehair nooses attached to a string, which is stretched over the ditches and canals used for irrigation, and so close to the water that the ducks are compelled when swimming under the string to stretch out their necks, when they are easily caught in the hanging nooses.

Also a useful plan for catching plovers or snipes, which haunt the edges of streams having a narrow margin between the bank and the water, is described by him as used for catching quails :

One method is simplicity itself : a hair noose is fastened to a lump of clay well worked together ; a number of these appliances are scattered about the lucerne fields, which the quails are fond of frequenting ; the bird caught in the noose is prevented from flying away owing to the weight of the lump of clay and its getting easily entangled in the grass.

Wheatears and ortolans are caught by suspending a hair noose between two turves placed on end and touching each other in the form of the roof of a house; to this shelter the birds constantly run on the approach of danger, or even, apparently, through timidity, on the gathering of storm clouds.

With this springe, also, thrushes and similar birds are described as being snared by Mr. Gould (in his "Birds of Great Britain"), who, giving Mr. Box as his authority, says :

The thrush is a great source of amusement to the middle, and of profit to the lower, classes during its autumnal migration. Many families of Liege, Luxemburg, Luneburg, Namur, parts of Hainault, and Brabant choose this season for their period of relaxation from business, and devote themselves to the taking of this bird with horsehair springes. The shopkeeper of Liege and Verviers, whose house in the town is the model of comfort and cleanliness, resorts with his wife and children to one or two rooms in a miserable country village to enjoy the sport he has been preparing with their help during the long evenings of the preceding winter, in the course of which he has made as many as from 5000 to 10,000 horsehair springes and prepared as many pieces of flexible wood, rather thicker than a swan-quill, in and on which to hang the birds. He hires what he calls his "tenderie," being from four to five acres of underwood about three to five years old, pays some thirty shillings for permission to place his springes, and his greatest ambition is to retain for several years the same tenderie and the same lodgings, which he improves in comfort from year to year. The springes being made and the season of migration near, he goes for a day to his intended place of sojourn, and cuts as many twigs, about 18in. in length, as he intends hanging springes. There are two methods of hanging them—in one the twig is bent into the form of the figure six, the tail end running through a slit cut in the upper part of the twig. The other method is to sharpen a twig at both ends, and insert the points into a grower or stem of underwood, thus forming a bow, of which the stem forms the string below the springe; and hanging from the lower part of the bow is placed a small branch, with three or four berries of the mountain ash (there called "sorbier"); this is fixed to the bow by inserting the stalk into a slit in the wood. The hirer of a new tenderie three or four acres in extent is obliged to make zigzag footpaths through it, to cut away the boughs which obstruct them, and even to hoe and keep them clean. Having thus prepared himself, he purchases one or two bushels of mountain ash berries, with the stalks to which they grow, picked for the purpose after they are red, but before they are ripe, to prevent falling off : these he lays out on a table in the loft or attic. The collection of these berries is a regular trade, and the demand for them is so great that, although planted expressly by the side of the roads in the Ardennes, they have been sold as high as £2 the bushel; but the general price is 5 francs. We will now suppose our thrush-catcher arrived at his lodgings in the country—that he has had his footpath cleared by the aid of a labourer, and that he is off for his first day's sport. He is provided with a basket, one compartment of which holds his twigs bent or straight, another his berries; his springes being already attached to the twigs, he very rapidly drives his knife into a lateral branch, and fixes them, taking care that the springe hangs neatly in the middle of the bow, and that the lower part of the springe is about three fingers' breadth from the bottom. By this arrangement the bird alighting on the lower side of the bow, and bending his neck to reach the berries below, places his head in the noose. Finding himself obstructed in his movements, he attempts to fly away; but the treacherous noose tightens round his throat, and he is found by the sportsman hanging by the neck, a victim of misplaced confidence.

The workman, who at this season earns a second harvest by this pursuit, carries on his industry in wilder districts, or he frequently obtains permission from his employer to set springes in his master's woods. In this case he supplies the family with birds, which are highly appreciated as a delicacy, especially when almost covered with butter, with a few juniper berries, and some bacon cut into small dice and baked in a pan. The rest of his take he sells at from 5d. to 10d. per dozen.

No person who has not lived in the country can imagine the excitement among all classes when the " grives " arrive. If the morning be foggy, it is a good day for " grives "; if bright, bad " tenderie "! The reason is obvious. When the birds arrive in a fog they settle at once in the woods ; if bright, they fly about, seeking the most propitious place for food.

It appears that redwings and fieldfares are caught by this method also, as well as a few ring-ousels and blackbirds.

" Stonehenge " says that the springe just described was used for snaring woodcocks, in the following manner :

It used to be the constant practice on all the hill downs in these parts to place cut underwood or furze, about a foot in height, to a very great extent along the ground, in the shape of a letter V, at the apex of which an opening would be left, where a hair noose or springe would be set, which seldom failed to yield the pot-hunter a nightly supply, as the cock would run along the side of the brushwood feeding, not taking the trouble to top over it, until he was led into the snare; but this plan is now, owing to the scarcity of cocks, when compared with former years, very seldom practised.

Ptarmigan are said by Daniels, in his " Rural Sports," to be led up to springes in nearly the same manner, stones being substituted for furze.

Another mode of making a springe, which is a capital plan for catching almost any bird, whether it be a percher or a runner, is this : Procure an elastic wand (hazel or osier makes the best) of about 3ft. 6in. long, to the top of which tie a piece of twisted horsehair about 3in. in length; to the free end attach a little piece of wood of 2in. in length, by the middle, cutting one end to an obtuse point, flattened on the top and underneath. Just underneath this little crosspiece attach two horsehair springes, at right angles; next cut a little fork, or rather angle piece, from a tree, one end of which is to be quite 4in. long (to drive in the ground), the other end about ½in., measuring from underneath. To set this trap, push the long wand into the ground until about 3ft. of it is out; then, at a distance of 2ft., drive in the fork piece, until only ½in. clears the ground; next bend the wand down in the form of a bow, and bring the pointed end of the crosspiece under the peg, or fork, planted in the ground at the other end. The free end is now a little elevated, while the middle is held very lightly on the point of

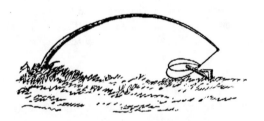

FIG. 2.—" SPRINGE," OR SNARE FOR BIRDS.

the catch, and its opposite end rests lightly on the ground. On the "ticklish" setting of this everything depends. Next place some blades of grass or light moss so as to hide the fork piece at the back and sides, taking care that no small sticks interfere with the proper working of the trap; strew some suitable seed or bait on the grass or moss, and then carefully place one horsehair noose in such a manner as to trap a bird should it merely hop on the crosspiece, and the other noose arrange so as to catch it by the neck should it attempt to seize the bait or to pass. In either case it dislodges the crosspiece, which instantly flies up, suspending the bird by the neck or legs in one or both of the nooses. The appearance of the set trap before the grass or moss is arranged is as represented in Fig. 2, which I have drawn from a trap set for that purpose. Sometimes this trap (or properly springe) is set with another fork placed at right angles to the other, and sufficiently distant from it to just catch the opposite end of the crosspiece, and though, perhaps, this plan allows it to be set a little finer, it has many disadvantages.

Yet another modification of the same springe. The wand or spring-stick, crosspiece, and nooses as before, but instead of the simple catch, use a complete bow, with both ends stuck in the ground. At some little distance from this drive in a straight piece of stick ; next procure a piece of stick with a complete fork or crutch at one end. To set it, draw down the spring-stick and pull the crosspiece under the bow by the top side farthest from the spring-stick. Now hold it firmly with one hand while

FIG. 3.—"SPRINGE" FOR SNIPE.

you place the forked stick with its crutch pressing against the opposite upright stick, and bring its free end against the lower end of the crosspiece, and adjust both as finely as you can. Finally, arrange the nooses in such a manner that if either of them or the crutched stick is touched the latter falls, and releasing the crosspiece, the spring-stick flies up, and the bird with it. To see the setting of this at a glance, *vide* Fig. 3 (showing only one noose, however), which I have "cribbed" from a tail piece of Bewick's, putting it a little out of drawing to show it up.

The next simple trap to be considered is evidently the pit-fall, used only, however, for large and fierce animals, and varying in construction in different countries. For descriptions of methods of baiting for and catching such animals as lions, leopards, tigers, elephants, &c., consult almost any book on African or Indian field sports.

Of poisons or intoxicants for capturing birds or animals, I do not intend to treat, as they are better left to gamekeepers and poachers.

Dead-falls, such as the "Figure of 4 trap," are easy to make, and useful for killing small animals. The materials required are simply three ordinary pieces of wood, a small piece of string, or, better still, wire, and a large, heavy, flat paving stone, or slate. Having procured three pieces of wood of half an inch square by one foot long, we call one the "upright," which is simply brought to a point at one end, somewhat like a chisel. The second is the "slanting stick," which should be cut to about

FIG. 4.—" FIGURE OF 4 " TRAP.

8in. long, having a nick in it about half an inch from one end, about half way through its depth; the other end is brought to a chisel point on its upper surface; the third, which is the "foot" or "bait stick," has a square notch, the thickness of the upright, cut in it, about three inches from one end; the inner end of this notch is relieved a little, so as not to bind on the upright too much. Within half an inch of the other end another notch is cut, but at right angles to the last, that is to say, this last notch is cut on the top, while the other is cut at the side; the outer or top notch also slopes inward. At the inner or side notch end drill a little hole, through which place a piece of pointed wire to receive the bait. The appearance of the three sticks when set is best explained by Fig 4; A is the

upright, B the slanting stick, and c bait or bottom stick. To
set it, take the upright in the left hand, chisel point up, pick
up B with the right hand, place it with its notch fitting on the
top of A, and keeping the slanting stick pressed down firmly,
you hold the two in proper position. This has relieved the left
hand entirely, which now is used to pick up c; place the side
notch of this on the upright A, slide it up until its end nick is
caught by the point of B; a sufficient leverage, as it were,
being attained on this, we can hold the whole of the trap now
with the right hand. By grasping B with the fingers of the
hand in opposition to the palm, while the thumb presses it down
on the top, the left hand, being at liberty, is used to drag the
stone and to raise one end to fall on the top of B; the weight of
the stone now sets the three parts in opposition to each other.
An animal touching the bait in the slightest manner is sufficient
to destroy the nice balance of the whole affair, and down it
comes with a run. The sizes given—from a trap I have just
set—are, of course, for small animals only, but it may be enlarged
or decreased to any extent, at the pleasure of the operator.

As "Stonehenge" and "High Elms" have introduced some
improvements, I may as well quote the former:

The Figure of 4 trap is composed of a large square piece of stone or
slate propped up in a peculiar manner with three pieces of wood, which
are arranged in the shape of a 4.

In examining this figure it will be seen to consist of a perpendicular
limb or upright, of a horizontal one or stretcher, and of a short slanting
stick, as the third is called. The upright is usually cut about half an
inch wide, shaved to a thin edge at top, but "High Elms" recommends
it to have a forked foot to keep it from twisting, and a notch in it to
prevent the stretcher slipping down. The slanting stick has a notch
cut in it half an inch from its upper end to receive the top of the upright,
while its lower end is shaved off to fit in a notch in the upper surface
of the front of the stretcher. Lastly, the stretcher has this notch in
front, and another notch cut in its side by which it is caught by the
upright and held in its place. A bait being tied to the external end of
the stretcher, and a stone placed so that it will lie flat on the ground,
the whole is ready for setting, which is effected as follows: Raise the
stone, and support it by the notched end of the slanting stick held
in the left hand, the notch itself looking downwards, then place the
upright with one end on the ground and the other in this notch, and

let it carry the weight of the stone, which will have a tendency to tilt up the slanting stick still held down by the left hand; finally, hitch the middle notch of the stretcher in the upright, with its front notch facing upwards, then bring the lower end of the slanting stick down to this front notch, drop it in, and the trap is set. Of course, it requires that each part shall be carefully adapted to the others, but when the trap is seen set it will be readily understood, practice being, however, required to set it properly. I quite agree with "High Elms" that the footed upright is an improvement; but I am inclined to doubt the advantage of the double notch between the upright and the stretcher. I have tried both, and I cannot find that there is any great superiority in his plan; but, perhaps, though I have exactly followed his directions as given in the *Field*, I may have omitted some point of practical importance. In setting the Figure of 4 trap, the height of the upright and the size and weight of the stone will be proportioned to the animal for which it is set. I do not like the trap myself, as it cannot be concealed so well as the steel trap, and, indeed, has no advantage except in cheapness. Dozens of them may be set in the woods, and if stolen little harm is done, as the cost is barely a penny apiece if made in large numbers. I have also known pheasants caught by the head and killed in them, the flesh with which they are baited being often attractive to tame-bred birds, which usually are fed with more or less of it in their rearing.

Mr. G. S. Purden has informed me that he has succeeded in capturing birds alive with this trap by hollowing out the ground where the stone falls.

Another "deadfall" for taking capercailzie in Norway is described by Mr. Yarrell in his "British Birds : "

Where the trees grow thickly on either side of a footpath, two long pieces of wood are placed across it; one end of these rests on the ground, the other being raised a foot and a half, or somewhat more, from the surface, and supported by a piece communicating with a triangular twig, placed in the centre of the path, and so contrived that on being slightly touched the whole fabric falls; a few stones are usually placed upon the long pieces of wood to increase the rapidity of the drop by the additional weight. Birds running along the footpath attempt to pass beneath the barrier, strike the twig, and are killed by the fall of the trap.

Taking birds by means of bird-lime is my next consideration. Bird-lime is made either from boiled oil or from holly-bark, but the making of it is not "worth the candle," it being so easily bought from any professional bird-catcher.

To those who wish to make their own, I commend the following : Take half a pint of linseed oil and put it into an old pot, or any vessel that will stand the fire without breaking. The vessel should not be more than one-third full. Place it over a slow fire and stir it until it thickens as much as required. This can be ascertained by cooling the stick in water and trying if it will stick to the fingers. When sufficiently boiled, pour into cold water, and it will be found ready for use.

I have submitted the foregoing to a practical birdcatcher and maker of bird-lime, and he has "passed" it as correct, only adding that the oil takes somewhere about four hours to slowly boil before it becomes sufficiently tenacious for use. Holly-bark he does not believe in, as he says it takes too long to make ; but that is no reason why we should pass over bird-lime made from this substance. The "Encyclopædia Britannica" says :

It is usually prepared by boiling holly-bark ten or twelve hours, and when the green coat is separated from the other it is covered up for a fortnight in a moist place; then pounded into a rough paste, and washed in a running stream till no motes appear. It is next put up to ferment for four or five days, and repeatedly skimmed. To prepare it for use, a third part of nut oil or thin grease must be incorporated with it over the fire.

Bird-lime can also be made from many other plants, but the best quality is made by either of the two methods mentioned above.

The "Edinburgh Encyclopædia" says further that—

When bird-lime is about to be applied to use, it should be made hot, and the rods or twigs should be warmed a little before they be dipped in it. Where straws and cords are to be limed it should be very hot, and after they are prepared they should be kept in a leather bag till used. In order to prevent bird-lime from being congealed by cold, it should be mixed with a little oil of petroleum; and, indeed, before the common kind can be used at all, it must be melted over the fire with a third part of nut oil or any thin grease, if that has not been added in the preparation. The smaller kinds of birds are frequently taken with bird-lime, which is one of the most eligible modes in frost or snow, when all sorts of small birds assemble in flocks, and which may be used in various ways. Put the bird-lime into an earthen dish, with the addition of one ounce of fresh lard to every quarter-pound of bird-lime, and melt the whole gently over the fire. Take a quantity of wheat ears, with a foot of the straw attached to them, and, having warmed the lime, that it may spread the thinner, lime about six inches of the straw from the bottom of the ears. Scatter a little chaff and thrashed ears over a compass of twenty yards; stick the limed straws into the ground, with the ears inclining downwards, or even touching the surface; traverse the adjoining places in order to disturb the birds, and make them fly towards the snare, and, by pecking at the ears of corn, they will become so entangled with the limed straw as to be easily taken by the hand. The lime may also be applied to cords, rods, and twigs, especially when it is intended to entangle the larger birds, such as snipes and fieldfares, and for this purpose the following mode may be adopted : Take the main branch of any bushy tree, with long, straight, and smooth twigs, such as the willow or birch, clear the twigs from every notch and prickle, lime the branches to within four fingers of the bottom, leaving the main bough from which the others rise untouched by the composition, and then place the bush where the birds resort. For small birds two to three hundred single twigs, about the thickness of a rush and three inches in length, may be stuck in sheaves of flag and corn. In hot and dry weather the twigs may be placed around the rivulets, ditches, and pools to which the birds come for drink, covering the waters at the same time with brushwood, so that they can have no access to quench their thirst, except at the spot where the twigs are fixed. For this purpose the rods or twigs should be about a foot in length, limed to within two inches of the thickest end, which is stuck into the bank in such a manner that they may lie within two fingers' breadth of the ground, and as the birds do not alight at once upon the place where they are to drink, but gradually descend from the higher trees to the lower, thence to the bushes, and lastly to the bank, it is useful to fix a few branches about a fathom from the water in a sloping direction, with a few lime twigs fastened upon them on which the birds will as frequently be caught as on those which are placed nearer to the water. The best time for this sport is from ten to eleven in the forenoon, from two to three in the afternoon, and about an hour before sunset, when the birds come to the watering places in flocks before they retire to roost.

The application of bird-lime is of ancient origin, and is practised in many countries. Pennant gives an account of how to take small birds by liming twigs around a stuffed or tethered live owl. I have heard of this plan being adopted, but have not tried it myself. From the curious manner in which small birds usually mob an owl, I should fancy it would succeed.

According to Folkard's " Wildfowler :"

There was also a method much in vogue previously to the invention and discovery of decoys, of taking wild fowl with lime strings made of packthread or string, knotted in various ways and besmeared with bird-lime ; these were set in rows about fens, moors, and other feeding haunts of the birds, an hour or two before morning or evening twilight. This plan was to procure a number of small stakes, about 2ft. in length, sharpened to a point at the nether end, and forked at the upper. These were pricked out in rows about a yard or two apart, some being placed in a slanting direction, and each stake siding one with another, within convenient distances of 4yds. or 5yds., so as to bear up the strings, which were laid upon the crutches, and placed loosely about 18in. above the ground. The lime strings were thus drawn from stake to stake in various directions, and lightly placed between the forks at the top of the stakes, some rows being higher than others ; and in this manner the whole space occupied by the stakes was covered with lime strings, as if carefully laid in wave-like coils, or placed in different directions, the ends being secured to the stakes with slip-knots, so that upon a light strain the whole of any string which might be touched by the bird became instantly loose, and, sticking to the feathers, the more it struggled to free itself, so much the more the string twisted about it, and thus the bird was quickly entangled, and became an easy prey. In this manner numbers of wild fowl of the largest species were taken at night at the moment of sweeping over the ground at very slow flight, just before alighting ; and it would appear that this method of fowling was particularly successful in taking plovers, which generally alight on the ground thickly congregated together.

A similar method was employed for taking wild fowl with lime strings placed over the surface of rivers and ponds frequented by those birds, and apparently with remarkable success. For this purpose it was necessary to procure a waterproof bird-lime wherewith to dress the strings, which were knotted in a similar manner to those employed for taking birds on land. The strings so prepared were in serpentine coils from stake to stake, the stakes being forked at the top, and of similar form to those last described, but of sufficient length to reach the bottom of the water and obtain a firm fixing in the mud. Some of the stakes were placed on the banks of the water or in any manner so that the lime strings could be drawn across and about the surface in different directions, resting here and there on some or other of the stakes or any boughs or overhanging trees, in such a way that the birds, when in the act of alighting on the water at night, might strike against the lime strings and become therein entangled.

The principal secret of success in this and the preceding device was that of placing the lime strings in shaded places over the most assured haunts of the birds; and it was only obtainable on dark nights, or in good shade, for whenever there was sufficient light for the birds to see the least sign of the snare spread for them the fowler had no chance of making any captives. (And be sure to take this caution not to use these strings in moonshine nights, for the shadow of the line will create a jealousy in the fowl, and so frustrate your sport.) And as wildfowl in their descent, just before alighting on the water, diverge from their accustomed angular figure, and spread themselves more in a broad front line, a whole flight sometimes comes swooping into the fowler's snare all at once.

A method of trapping, with the assistance of bird-lime, might, I think, be tried with some chance of success. It is to insert a piece of fish in a cone of paper well smeared with bird-lime, and to throw down a few of these prepared cones in places accessible to gulls, herons, and such birds, who, in attempting to seize the fish, would be effectually hoodwinked, and thus easily secured.

Hawking, by which birds are captured by trained falcons, is of the highest antiquity. Pennant mentions that the Saxon King Ethelbert (who died in 760) sent to Germany for a cast of falcons to fly at cranes (herons?). As this sport has now fallen into disuse, I must refer my readers for particulars to Blaine, Daniel, Freeman, Harting, Captain Dugmore, and to occasional articles by one or two modern falconers in the columns of the *Field*.

The infinite variety of nets used in the capture of various birds requires almost a chapter by itself; but it will suffice for the present one if we mention those most generally used, or the most striking varieties. First, then, comes the ordinary "clap-net" of the London and provincial bird-catchers. The "Edinburgh Encyclopædia" says, with regard to clap-nets:

Birds are also taken with nets during the day, and especially in those seasons of the year when they change their situation ; in the month of October, for instance, when the wild birds begin to fly, and in March, when the smaller kinds assemble for pairing. They are chiefly on the wing from daybreak to noon, and always fly against the wind. The birdcatchers, therefore, lay their nets towards that point to which the wind blows. The nets employed in this way are generally 12½yds. long and 2½yds. wide, and are spread on the ground parallel to each other, in such a manner as to meet when turned over. They are provided with lines, fastened in such a way that, by a sudden pull, the birdcatcher is able to draw them over the birds that may have alighted in the space between those parallel sides. In order to entice the wild birds to alight amongst the nets, *call birds* are employed, of which there must be one or two of each of the different kinds which are expected to be caught, such as linnets, goldfinches, greenfinches, &c. Besides the *call birds* there are others denominated *flur birds*, which are placed upon a moveable perch within the net, called a *flur*, and which can be raised or depressed at pleasure, and these are secured to the *flur* by means of a brace or bandage of slender silk strongly fastened round the body of the bird. The call birds are deposited in cages at a little distance from the nets, and as soon as they see or hear the approach of the wild birds, which they perceive long before it can be observed by the birdcatcher, they announce the intelligence from cage to cage with the greatest appearance of joy, and they proceed to invite them to alight by a succession of notes or short jerks, as they are termed by the birdcatcher, which may often be heard at a considerable distance. The moment that the call is heard by the wild birds they stop their flight and descend towards the net, and so great is the ascendancy and fascination of the call birds that they can induce the others to return repeatedly to the nets till every bird in the flock be caught.

Being somewhat afraid that this description would not meet all the practical requirements of the case, and knowing myself but little or nothing of this mode of birdcatching, I thought it advisable to interview a practical man. Having at last succeeded in capturing a specimen of the *genus homo*, species birdcatcher, I prevailed upon him (through the medium of a tip) to impart his stock of birdcatching lore, and to cut me patterns of play-sticks and pegs, and also to correct my rough sketches when necessary.

The sum and substance of my interview is as follows : The nets, which are of two pieces, are each about twelve yards long by two-and-a-half yards wide, and are made with a three-quarter mesh of what is technically called two-thread. The staves at each end, to which the nets are permanently attached, are made of red deal, ferruled and jointed at the middle, in the manner of a fishing rod, for the convenience of carriage. The length of each when put together is about five feet six inches, being thus shorter than the width of the net. This, it will be readily observed, allows for the bagging of the net —an important particular, as, if the nets were strained tight with no allowance made for bagging, the birds would flutter along the ground until they got out at one end or the other. As it is, they roll themselves up in the meshes, and effectually entangle themselves while attempting to escape.

A strong line, called the top line, made of clock line, passes the whole length of each net, and is protracted some feet past the staves at either end. A similar line runs along the bottom made of three-thread or whip thread. This is called the bottom line. There are then two unattached cords of some strength, called the pull line and the forked line, which latter is attached, when required for use, to the two staves nearest the birdcatcher, at the intersection of the top line.

Eight pegs are used, made of hard wood, generally ash, four of which are called the "chief pegs." The whole of the pegs are notched, for the convenience of attaching a line.

The method of laying the clap-net is best described with the aid of a drawing (*vide* Fig. 5).

The first thing to be done is to lay down the right-hand net, and to drive in the two chief pegs where shown, namely, at the bottom of the staves, to which they are attached by a loop of strong cord, acting as a hinge. The two end pegs are then driven in the ground at some little distance from and in an exact line to the chief pegs. The bottom line is then made fast at each end, as also the continuation of the top line. The two pegs, lines, and staff thus form a triangle at each end. The other net is then laid in such a manner that when both are pulled over, one net shall overlap the other to the extent of six inches. It is then turned back and pegged down in the same way as the right-hand net. The next operation is to tie the forked line to each top end

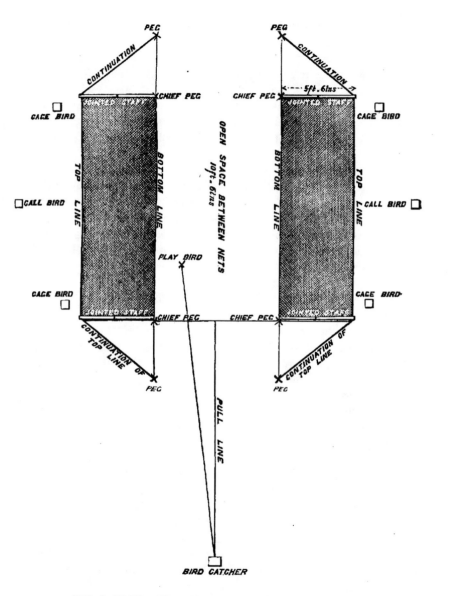

FIG. 5.—PLAN AND METHOD OF SETTING CLAP-NET.

of the staves, a nick being cut in each for this purpose. Exactly in the centre of the forked line the pull line is knotted, at the other end of which the birdcatcher stands at varying distances, according to the bird he wishes to catch; for instance, for linnets or goldfinches, thirty to forty yards; for starlings a greater distance is required; or to capture these wary birds a better plan is to place the nets in one field while you retire into another, bringing the pull line through an intervening hedge.

Cages containing birds are dispersed about on the outer edges of the nets, the best, or call birds, being placed farther away; in fact, my informant thinks that if all the cages were placed a moderate distance away from the nets it would be better, as he has found that the usual red or green cages have been the means of "bashing"—i.e., frightening—the wild birds away from the nets.

"When doctors differ, who shall decide?"

On mentioning the above to another birdcatcher he gave a huge snort of dissatisfaction, and roundly swore that my man knew "nought about it," for *he* always set his cages as near the nets as possible; "for don't it stand to reason," quoth he, "that if you set your cages fur away, your 'call birds' will 'tice the wild 'uns down round 'em? an' they won't come near your nets."

An important actor in the performance is the "play-bird," which is a bird braced by a peculiar knot or "brace," as shown in Fig. 6, on an arrangement called the play-stick.

The "play-stick" is resolvable into three parts, Fig. 7 being the ground peg, formed of a piece of hard wood about six inches long, having a round hole bored through close to the top, through which the "play-line" passes. Immediately underneath is a square slot for the reception of a piece of brass tube beaten flat at one end (Fig. 8), while the other end is left open for the reception of the "play-stick" (C, Fig. 9), simply a rough twig or piece of hard wood, upon which the bird is tied by the "brace" (Fig. 6)—which is constructed, as shown in drawing, by doubling a piece of string, tying a knot in the centre and then joining the ends. The head and body of the bird is thrust through, so that a loop catches it on each side and in front of the wings, the legs and tail being thrust through the other, one loop coming on each side of the body behind the wings. A swivel is attached at one of the knots, and, by another piece of string, is made fast to the play-stick near its end. The bird is thus perfectly free so far as the wings and legs are concerned.

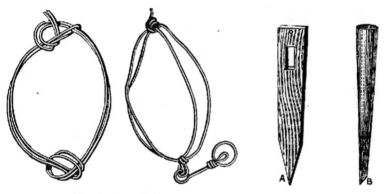

FIG. 6.—BIRD BRACE.
Detail showing   Complete, with Swivel
Formation of Knots.   attached.

FIG. 7.   FIG. 8.
GROUND PEG.   TUBE OF PLAY-STICK.

The "play-stick," as a whole, is represented in Fig. 9, which shows the bird in repose, with the end of the stick (C,) resting on the ground, the play-line passing through a hole in the ground peg (A), while the part marked B works in the slot in the same.

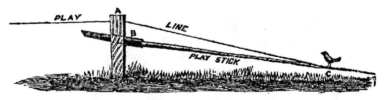

FIG. 9.—" FLUR " OR " PLAY-STICK "

A little food and water are put down by the play-bird's side, to which it addresses itself in its intervals of rest. Directly birds appear, the play-line is smartly pulled, which has the effect of jerking the play-bird upwards, while at the same time it flutters its wings to regain its perch. This motion is mistaken by the wild birds as a natural proceeding; they accordingly alight around the play-bird, to assist it in feeding. The pull-line of the net is then smartly jerked, which causes the forked-line to fly inwards, and, acting on the hinged pegs and top and bottom lines as by a lever, the staves rise from the outside, become perpendicular, and finally fall over, inclosing all within the open space in the nets.

The "play-bird" is alway placed on the left hand of the birdcatcher, about two yards into the net. Sometimes more than one play-stick and bird are used; all are, however, played by the same string. The best birds are, however, contrary to my expectations, not used, as the constant pulling up and down, to say nothing of the worry of the falling nets, very soon kills the poor little "play-bird." From Michaelmas to Christmas would appear to be the best times for catching.

Many rare birds not calculated on by the operator, are procured in this way. I allude to hawks, which constantly dash at the call, or play-birds, of the netsman. I remember seeing, taken in a lark net on the racecourse of Corfu—one of the Ionian Isles—a most beautiful male specimen of the hen harrier (*Circus cyaneus*, Macg.); and here in England I have received, within the last few years, one great grey shrike (*Lanius excubitor*, L.), four or five hobby hawks (*Falco subbuteo*, L.), a dozen or more merlins (*Falco æsalon*, Tunstall), and a great number of sparrowhawks, and kestrels, all captured by this method.

Draw-nets are those used by fen-men and others at night for taking lark, snipe, plover, &c., by dragging a long net of a certain construction over the fields and swamps. The actual originator of this method of capture as applied to snipe and such birds, appears to have been Mr. Daniel himself (*vide* "Rural Sports," vol. 3, p. 179).

Glade nets, which are nets stretched in narrow glades or ridings in woods from tree to tree, are used chiefly for taking night-flying birds, such as woodcocks, or wild ducks. Folkard thus describes their use:

The proceedings connected with the use of glade nets appear to be very simple. These nets are of lengths and breadths proportioned to the places in which they are suspended. They are simply pieces of fine thread netting, edged with cords adapted to the extent of the lint. The glade net so formed is suspended between two trees, directly in the track of the woodcock's flight. Both the upper and lower corners have each a rope attached to them which, as regards the upper part of the net, is rove through sheaves, iron rings, or thimbles fastened to the trees on either side at the top of the glade at a moderate height, varying from ten to twelve or fifteen feet. The falls of the two upper ropes are joined or so adjusted that they form a bridge, to the central part of which a rope is attached of several yards in length, which the fowler holds in his hand in a place of concealment, and thus commands full power over the net, being able to drop it down suddenly and intercept the flight of any birds which may attempt to escape through the glade ; or he can draw it up as suddenly from the ground to a perpendicular position. A stone, of about 5lb. weight, is attached to each of the lower cords of the net, so that when the fowler lets go his controlling rope the weight of the stones forces the lower part of the net down in an instant with a strong fall, and, at the same time, they draw up the upper part of the net. The fowler having stationed himself in such a position as to command a full view of the glade in which his net is placed, beaters are employed to flush the cocks from their retreats ; immediately on one or more flying in the direction of the fowler a signal is given, and just as the bird approaches the net it is suddenly let down or drawn up, when the woodcock, flying forcibly against it, is immediately ensnared. The instant the birds have struck the net the fowler lets go another rope, which is generally looped to a stake within reach of his arm, and the whole net, with the birds entangled, then drops to the ground. In forcing themselves forward in their endeavour to escape they form the net into a sort of bag, which makes their capture more certain.

Nets are in some parts of the world set under water to procure wild fowl. I remember, when in Norfolk, a gannet being brought in by one of the fishing boats ; the bird had become accidentally entangled in one of the nets whilst attempting to rob it of some fish.

Small nets of a few yards long, made of fine black silk, with a small mesh, are used in some parts of the country for taking kingfishers. These nets are stretched across a small watercourse or the arch of a bridge in such a manner that, a little "slack" being allowed, the bird is taken to a certainty in attempting to pass. So fatal is this net when skilfully set, that

I know one man who adds several pounds to his income in the course of a year by taking kingfishers in this manner.

For the netting of hawks by a contrivance called the bow net, which was formerly used in England, see Blaine's "Encyclopædia of Rural Sports."

Many birds (notably sea and rock birds) are to be procured by descending the rocks attached to a stout line. But this highly dangerous work had better not be attempted by the tyro. For an ancient but interesting account of rock fowling in the Orkneys, see Pennant's "Arctic Zoology," page 29. The same system is still adopted on many parts of the coast. In fact, I recollect (when some years ago I visited the Isle of Wight on a collecting expedition) seeing two men with ropes and an iron bar going to the top of the " Bench " (a famous place for sea fowl), and while one man was let down over the edge of the cliff his fellow remained at the top to answer the pull of the " bird-line " and look after the safety of the " man-rope " and iron bar. So fascinating did this appear to me that, having been " between heaven and earth " once or twice before, I volunteered to " go below ; " but I found that the fowlers did not care for the risk, or the loss of time, and booty, involved in letting an amateur down.

It was, indeed, a wonderful sight. I crept as closely as I dared, and lying on my breast looked over the cliff. Hundreds of feet down, the sea, lashed into breakers by the breeze, crept up the steep black rock walls, or tumbled over the half-hidden crags ; and yet, though you could see the white war of waters, but the faintest murmur of this battle between land and sea could be heard—below and halfway up, the puffins and guillemots were sitting in rows, or flying off in droves as little black specks on the white foam.

Here I learned that they often baited fish-hooks with offal or pieces of fish, for the purpose of catching the gulls, and this brought to my mind the quantities of robins, thrushes, and such birds I had seen caught by fish-hooks baited with worms and pegged down in the olive groves of the Ionian Sea.

I notice that Pennant mentions that the lapwing is decoyed into nets by the twirling of looking glass. I have seen exactly the same thing myself on the Continent applied to the taking of larks. A cylinder of wood, inlaid with pieces of looking-glass, is fixed between two uprights, and made to revolve by means of a small crank and wheel, to which a line is attached. The netsman, retiring to some little distance, keeps the cylinder in constant motion by pulling the line, at the same time keeping up a soft whistling noise with his mouth. The larks flutter over the twirler, and seemingly dazzled, descend on the ground between the nets which are then pulled over in the usual manner.

Steel traps are of many shapes and sizes, and are best procured ready made from a good firm, though I have known a few country blacksmiths who could turn them out decently. As everyone knows this, the ordinary " gin," or tooth trap, used for capturing rats or other animals and birds, no description is, I think necessary, further than to say that the springs should be highly tempered, and that the teeth should not be too long. These traps can be set in various places with or without baits— in the water, on the ground, up a tree, or on a post; but post-traps proper, which are chiefly useful, when set unbaited, for catching hawks, are made with an arm and spring at right angles to the plate, so that they may be fastened to the post which supports them. In setting these traps great care and skill are necessary; and in giving directions how to do this properly, I cannot do better than quote "Stonehenge," who says :

First lay the trap on the ground, then mark the outline of it, allowing half an inch clear all round; cut away the turf to this pattern, and in the centre dig a hole deep enough to receive a strong peg and the chain which fastens the trap to it, which will thus be entirely concealed; drive in the peg, arrange the chain neatly upon this and in the channel for the spring, and then set the trap in its place, temporarily propping up the plate by a piece of twig, which can finally be withdrawn by a string; take care so to cut away the turf that the jaws are only just below the level of the ground. Having done this, cut a very thin slice of the turf which was removed to make way for the trap, leaving little more than the grass itself with a ragged edge, and lay this gently on the plate, and withdraw the prop. Then cover the spring in the same way; and, lastly, put some more shreds of grass or leaves over the jaws themselves, but in such a way that the former will not be caught between the teeth when the trap is sprung. When the keeper can do all this so neatly that the trap cannot be discovered by the eye at two or three yards distance, and yet will be sprung by half an ounce weight being placed upon the plate over and above what it has already, and without leaving anything between the jaws, he may be considered a master of his craft. All this should be done with strong leather gloves on the hands, and with as little breathing over the trap as possible. The object of these precautions is to avoid leaving any scent behind, which might alarm the vermin, who are always suspicious of any place where they have reason to believe man has been at work.

Daniel, in his " Rural Sports," says :

Otters are taken in an unbaited trap, for they reject every kind of bait, This trap must be placed near his landing place, which will be found by carefully examining the edges of rivers or ponds, either by his spraints, his seal, or the remains of fish (for in whatever place he eats his plunder he always leaves the tail or hinder parts of the fish undevoured). The trap must be set in and covered with mud to prevent his seeing it ; the instant the trap "strikes," the otter plunges into the water with it, when its weight, preventing his rising to the surface, soon destroys him. The trap will seldom be drawn more than twenty yards from the spot, and with a grappling iron is soon recovered. If the place where he comes out of the water cannot be discovered, upon the ground where the remains of fish are left, cut a hole near the edge of the water, and place a trap or two upon a level with the ground and cover it over carefully with moss.

This aqueous method of trapping, is also recommended for taking all birds of the crow tribe. The bait in this case is an egg, so secured that on the bird walking along a prepared pathway to seize the delicacy he springs a concealed trap, and fluttering into deep water drowns by the weight of the attachment.

Another method of setting the trap on land for the taking of some animals, which, says Daniel, speaking of the marten (now a rare animal in most parts of England), is a sure way of catching this destructive little animal in a park or covert which is railed in, is to cut a groove in some of the posts or gate posts, in which set an unbaited steel trap, and as they constantly run along the posts and pales early in the morning to dry themselves, in leaping up from the ground upon the place where the trap is set, they are sure to be captured.

Fish is recommended as bait for weasels, polecats, &c.,

although I think the best way of trapping such animals is to form an enclosure of brushwood, &c., in which peg down some live bird, leading two narrow pathways from it from each end and exactly opposite each other, in each of which place an ordinary steel trap, unbaited, concealed in as skilful a manner as possible. The animal running along one of these pathways, to seize his prey, is inevitably trapped. Be sure and have two openings, or this plan will not succeed. Cats may be trapped in this manner.

St. John, in his "Highland Sports," mentions that if a wild cat, or fox, can be killed, and the body placed in the usual haunts of its kind, well surrounded with traps, curiosity or some such feeling will impel them to visit the "dear departed," and in walking round they often succeed in springing the traps, and remaining as mourners in a fashion they did not intend.

Hawks may be trapped by first capturing their young, and pegging one or more to the ground, and surrounding it or them by concealed traps. This cruel but highly effective way succeeds by reason of the old birds seeing or hearing their young, and attempting to release them.

If part of a bird or animal killed by a hawk can be found, a good plan is to allow it to remain, surrounding it also with concealed traps, as they usually return to finish their meal, and that sometimes after the lapse of days.

The "box trap" is used for catching many animals for which the ordinary gin is used; but the advantage which it possesses over the latter is that it captures all animals alive, which, in the case of a hare or a rabbit accidentally getting in, is of consequence, as it may be released unhurt, whereas the ordinary steel trap, if accidentally sprung by them, would have killed or maimed them to a certainty. These box traps can be bought ready-made at many places; but, for those who wish to make one themselves, I must refer them for plans and description to Col. Hawker, or "Stonehenge." Almost anything does to bait a gin or box trap with—bits of flesh, fish, offal, half-cooked red herrings, &c.—and it is a generally understood thing that if half-putrid flesh or entrails of any animal are rubbed over traps or the thorns or bushes placed as entrances to traps, hares and the like will seldom go near.

Of course, a very small trap must be used for small birds, and baited either with seeds, bread, worms, or a small piece of fat meat, which latter is a most tempting bait for the birds of the genus *Parus* (titmice).

There are several other made traps, such as the trap cage; the best of which has a bird as a decoy partitioned off from the actual trap. This is a useful little trap in some seasons, and is well known, being easily procurable at any of the bird fanciers'.

Mr. James Hiam, well known in Worcestershire for his "Notes on Natural History," sends me the following description of his method of trapping bullfinches:

I find the best way to trap bullfinches is to procure a caged bird, also what is known as a trap-cage, putting the tame bird in the lower part, placing a bunch of blackberries or privet berries in the top part; and hanging the cage against a wall or tree out of the reach of cats. I have reserved a stock of bunches of blackberries by inserting their stems in water, grape-fashion, for a succession of food for bait. I have also caught scores, if not hundreds, on bird-lime, but this injures their plumage and is somewhat troublesome, especially to anyone not accustomed to handle it. I have also caught them in a bat fowling net at night out of thick hedges. I find a trap cage or cages best, for bullfinches generally go in small parties, and I have taken two out at once from two separate cages, while others waited round and were caught afterwards.

The well-known and easily imitated call of the bullfinch at this season of the year (autumn) appears to have a greater attraction—for what reason I cannot say—than at any other period; there is also a great difference in individual call birds. The best should be selected. When fresh caught, bullfinches are best placed in a low kind of box cage about six inches deep, with wires only on one side. Such cage may be easily made out of a soap box from the grocer's, giving them a good supply of canary and hemp seed and water. If they refuse to eat the seed, which sometimes happens, give a few blackberries or such other food as they feed on at the time; the seed of the dock is always a favourite dish in the winter, and the probability is in a day or two they will take to the seed, which should be strewed over the bottom of the cage.

The nightingale trap (perhaps not quite so well known) is a compromise between the bow net and the spring trap; it is useful for taking most insectivorous birds, is easily made by anyone possessing a little mechanical ability, and is to be bought cheaply at most of the bird shops. As I have been asked, however, by many correspondents in the country, where such things are to be procured, they are informed that in the classic retreat of the Seven Dials—that is to say, in the street running through from Charing Cross to Bloomsbury—are to be found many bird fanciers' shops where the nightingale trap can be procured for something under a couple of shillings.

In setting all of these traps be sure to touch them with the hands as little as possible, especially if setting a baited trap. Gloves are recommended to be worn, scented with musk when baiting for stoats, weasels, &c., and with vervain or valerian if baiting for cats.

I will proceed now to the consideration of decoys. Decoys are of two classes, fixed and mechanical, or those easily removable and natural. Of the former the most important is what is called a decoy for wild fowl, viz., a large tract of land and water specially fitted up with nets of the sorts most suitable for taking ducks and similar birds, and near which it is unlawful to fire a gun. For a thoroughly exhaustive and interesting article on decoy ponds, see Folkard's "Wild Fowler," pp. 44—94.

Some singular and highly original methods of catching birds are described by ancient and modern authors. Pennant, in his "Arctic Zoology," vol. ii, page 550, describes a quaint but doubtful method of decoying wild geese in Siberia; he also, at page 311, records how immense numbers of willow grouse are taken by a curious mode of netting.

Folkard also mentions an ingenious way of capturing wild fowl in their own element by the aid of calabashes. This, however, I think, "must be seen to be believed," though I am bound to confess that it is partly corroborated by other writers.

Of the lasso or the "bolas," used in South America for capturing certain animals and birds, no description need be given, as this method of trapping is only to be performed by a person trained from childhood to ride and throw the lasso. The same remark applies to the use of the blowpipe (see Bates's "Amazons"), and the Australian "boomerang" and "throwstick." Regarding the use of the blowpipe, I see that an American author on Taxidermy, who has written a very good book on the subject—albeit he has, perhaps unwittingly, cribbed my title of "Practical Taxidermy"—appears to have attained remarkable proficiency in the use of this weapon, and describes also his method of making it, thus :

The blowpipe is of great service for collecting warblers and other small birds. It should be made by encasing a long glass tube in wood, to prevent breaking. The ordinary glass tubes used by glass-blowers make good blowpipes, which should have a diameter of ½in. and be not less than 6ft. long.

To encase a pipe with wood, take two strips of straight-grained pine, and plane or "gouge" out a half-round groove the full length of each, glue them together, and wire firmly over the glass pipe. When the glue is dry, remove the wires, and plane the wood round until it has a diameter of 1¼in.; if smaller it will sag, and not do good shooting. Putty balls should be used, and blown with a quick puff, which is easily acquired by practice. The putty is thickened with whiting until the pellets will roll hard, but they should not be dry enough to crumble.

With this novel gun I have killed as many as fifty-six warblers in less than a day, and spoiled but few specimens in killing.

Rowland Ward, also, in his "Sportsman's Handbook," appears to favour the use of the blowpipe, and very correctly says at page 9 :

The implement is so simple and so easily constructed that the price of it is inappreciable. About 3ft. length of any straight metal or wooden tubing, ¾in. diameter, through which a pellet the size of a marble may be thrown, will serve well, but an even longer tube may be chosen. The pellet should be of clay or any putty, rolled in the hand to easily pass through the barrel without too much windage. It should not touch the mouth, but be lightly placed just in the orifice, by stopping which with the thumb the tube can be conveniently carried loaded, muzzle up, ready for the most rapid use. To propel the pellet the puff must be sudden and powerful. There is a proper way of effecting this. When a practitioner first begins to use the blow-pipe, it is a common error to eject the breath only direct from the lungs ; he should acquire the habit of inflating his cheeks, so as to make a storage of wind, as it were, for each shot; that, added to the breath from the lungs, gives a force which will sometimes astonish him. The hand follows the eye in aim, and practice will often develop unthought-of proficiency.

The catapult is also a first-rate weapon in a skilful hand for procuring small birds. I must confess I cannot use it as well as some young friends of mine, who knock over nearly every sitting bird they aim at, and even now and then are successful with such difficult shots as at swallows on the wing; a novice, on the contrary, nearly always succeeds in stinging his fingers and missing the object aimed at.

I remember also, when a boy, using a very effective weapon, which I should describe as a catapult gun. It was, if I recollect aright, fashioned similarly to a cross bow, the bolt, however, from which was ejected from a little wash-leather bag by means of very powerful india-rubber springs, which being released by a trigger delivered a bullet or small shot from a tube with amazing force and precision. I do not know if such guns are made now, but I should imagine that anyone with a little ingenuity could construct one for himself.

All these appliances, with the well-known air-gun, are chiefly of use for collecting the smaller birds with a minimum of noise. There are several small collecting guns made which do the work required in a much more thorough manner. Messrs. Bland, gun-makers, of Birmingham, some time since showed me an elegant little double-barrelled central fire gun, which seems to be just the thing for the purpose. Messrs. Clarke, of Leicester, also make a small single-barrelled central fire ·410-bore collector's gun, but as before observed, they are only fit for small birds at short ranges.

I have lately procured a small walking-stick gun ·410-bore, central fire, with a removeable stock, which I have found of great service in collecting small birds—bringing down swifts and swallows flying, at moderate ranges.

Many birds, especially males, in the breeding season, are taken by decoying them into nets or snares by tame or wild birds of the opposite sex; in fact, advantage was wont to be taken of the pugnacity or devotion of the Ruffes when "hilling," by previously setting springes or nets on their battle-ground, into which said snares they danced, when courting or fighting (see Daniel, vol. iii., p. 212).

Poachers also sometimes take cock pheasants by bringing an armed gamecock into the woods and hiding themselves, while the domesticated bird challenges and gives battle to the unarmed wild one. The boldness of cock pheasants during their breeding time is wonderful; many instances having come under my notice of wild pheasants coming from the woods to do battle with aviary ones, and also with farm-yard " roosters."

A highly interesting account of the ludicrous actions and insensibility to fear of the capercailzie, and blackgame, when courting (and through which they are easily shot), is given by a writer on Norway in the *Field* of March 27, 1875; and this brings us to the greatest of all aids for the procuring of specimens—I mean the shot-gun and rifle. So much of success depends upon being a clever marksman, and also upon having a good general knowledge of woodcraft, that although for instructions in guns and shooting I refer the reader to Col. Hawker, Daniel, Blaine, " Stonehenge," Folkard, Greener, " Wildfowler," and many others, yet a few words on some peculiar, and in some cases well-known, methods of decoying birds within gun-shot, may not be out of place.

The stalking-horse was, no doubt, the earliest decoy or shield under which the ancient fowler got near his birds with the cross-bow or gun. It was sometimes a mere framework of wood, covered with painted canvas to represent a horse or cow, or was a real animal trained to feed and move in a natural manner in the midst of the fowl. In the first instance, the fowler carried the framework in front of him, and made his shot through an opening; in the second case he gently urged the animal on, hiding behind, and making his shot under the belly, or over the back. For ancient methods of stalking, see Gervase Markham; for a modern method, see "Bustard Shooting in Spain," in the *Country* of Jan. 21, 1875, and current pages of the *Field*.

Decoying birds by imitating their notes or cries is an art which the collector must acquire. Many mechanical calls for wood pigeons, curlews, and other birds are made. One call, which I do not think is made or used in England,* is a Greek idea for decoying thrushes. It is a whistle formed from two discs of thin silver or silvered copper, each the size of, or a little

---

* Since writing this I find there are now sold to boys, for the large sum of one-halfpenny, whistles formed in tin, of almost similar construction to those described. I never yet found anyone to make them " speak " properly; boys not knowing how to modulate or *inspire* the breath. I have now tried one of them against my silver whistle, and I cannot say which has the better tone.

smaller than, a "graceless" florin, or say an inch across; these discs are—one fully concave, and the other slightly convex, both have a hole in the centre and are soldered together by their edges in the manner shown in Fig. 10. The concave part is placed in the mouth, pressing against the teeth, and by inspiring the breath and modulating the tones with the closed or open hands, as the case may be, a very perfect imitation of the song-thrush's note is the result. This, the arriving or newly-arrived birds

FIG. 10.—DECOY WHISTLE FOR THRUSHES, &c.

hear, and, imagining it proceeds from the throat of one of their species, who, entirely at his ease, is letting the ornithological world know how excessively overjoyed he is at his safe arrival, alight in the trees which surround and conceal the treacherous imitator, and quickly fall a prey to the ready gun. So infatuated are they, that enormous quantities are killed by this method early in the season; in fact, I knew one person who shot one hundred and four, besides other birds, to his own gun in one day.

Quails may be called from a distance if the sportsman hides himself and imitates with his mouth their peculiar cry, "More wet, more wet."

There are many other birds which come to call in addition to quail. Woodpigeons and doves will sometimes be attracted to an ambush by making a soft cooing noise with the mouth and the hollows of both hands, but the most successful way of procuring both of these birds is to build a hut with boughs in the hedge of a field to which they resort, in which hut the shooter hides himself, keeping perfectly quiet, and not attempting to shoot until the birds have begun feeding, as woodpigeons, or doves, when they first alight "have their eyes all about them," the slight rustle even of the gun being brought to the present, is enough to scare them, and a snap shot at a flying dove is rarely successful when you are penned and cramped up in a little bough hut. Pea, tare, and barley fields, when they are first sown in the spring, and pea and corn fields, after getting in the crops in the autumn, are their especial haunts, though they do not despise turnip leaves and acorns. Salt marshes are also especially favoured by all the pigeon family in quest of salt, of which they seem to be inordinately fond. Fresh water rivers in hot weather are also sure spots to find them; and a stuffed pigeon is a good decoy in some seasons, if placed in front of a place of concealment.

Perhaps it may be as well to mention that often, while lying in wait for wild pigeons, you will observe the advent of one or two tame ones, or even a flock from some neighbouring farmyard, and, as some of these pigeons are almost certain to closely resemble the wild stock dove (*Columba œnas*, L.), some little discrimination is required to distinguish the two species.

The Gannet or Solan goose (*Sula bassana*, Hewitson) is said to be taken by the strange device of floating a plank out at sea, to which a fish is attached, in such a manner that, on the bird dashing down on the half-submerged plank, it strikes itself with such violence as not unfrequently to break its neck or breastbone. On mentioning this to Mr. Frederick Ryland, he assured me that he has in some instances observed the marks of the bird's bill, which had indented the plank—a pretty conclusive evidence of the extraordinary force of its descent.

Many other birds besides pigeons are attracted by "stales," which was the ancient name for a representation of the living bird by stuffed specimens or wooden images; knots and godwits, says Daniel (vol. iii., p. 214), were attracted into nets by this mode. Gulls and terns I have often found attracted by a stuffed bird, or, when one can be shot, should it be left to lie on the water, or propped up on land, as if alive, the others almost always hover around it. Sheep's lights thrown on the water is another good decoy for gulls. Ducks are sometimes attracted by dummies of indiarubber sold at some of the shops for that purpose, but the best modification of this is the French "hut system," described at length, in his

E

usual amusing style, by the once-renowned Col. Hawker. A more singular way still, of decoying these birds to the gun is by the American fashion of "toling," a lucid description of which I append, culled from the pages of Folkard's "Wildfowler:"

There is one system of fowling practised in America which is as curious in performance as it is interesting. It is probably one of the most remarkable methods ever invented, and approaches the nearest to the system of decoy as practised in England of any of the arts employed by the people of a foreign country for the capture of wildfowl. The method alluded to is termed "toling." I am unable to trace the origin of the term, unless it simply implies a death knell, for such it assuredly assumes to those birds which approach within range of the secreted sportsman.* This singular proceeding is said to have been first introduced upwards of fifty years ago near Havre-de-Grace, in Maryland; and, according to traditional testimony, the art was accidentally discovered by a sportsman whilst patiently lying in ambush watching a paddling of wild ducks, which were a little beyond the range of his gun. Whilst in a state of doubt and anxiety as to whether they would approach near enough to be shot, he suddenly observed them raise their heads and swim towards the shore apart from his ambuscade; and, whilst wondering at the cause of so strange a proceeding, his attention was directed to a fox which was skipping about on the shore, and evidently enticing the ducks to approach. This accidental discovery of so weak a point in the nature of the feathered tribe led the sportsman to turn it to advantage, and thence arose the curious art of "toling." To practise it successfully the sportsman requires simply the services of a dog, which he uses in a similar way to that of a "piper," employed at an English decoy.

For the purpose of "toling," the American sportsman erects blinds or screens on the margin of some lake, the resort of wildfowl; when any birds are in sight upon the water, he, with his dog, takes up a position behind the screens, and by throwing small bits of wood or pebbles up and down the shore, he keeps the dog in active motion so as to attract the attention of the birds, and induce them to swim towards the shore within a few yards of the screens, when, if they do, the sportsman immediately discharges his fowling piece at them, and sometimes kills large numbers at a shot. The principal things to be observed are, a strict silence, and to keep the dog constantly in motion, and all the time in sight of the

---

* The word "toling" may be explained as a corruption of "tolling," *i.e.*, enticing.

ducks. The little animal should be encouraged to skip and bound over the rocks and stones in front of the screens, and to flourish his tail about with playful vivacity. He must never bark, for that would alarm the fowl and cause them to fly away immediately.

Red or chestnut coloured dogs with long bushy tails are best for the purpose of "toling"; the nearer they approach a fox in colour and appearance the better.

Tubs may be sunk on the seashore into which the shooter gets at the approach of night (or even a "skip" or basket may be used to sit on) to wait till flight time to procure specimens; but having myself sat in a marsh at night between a river and the sea in Norfolk more than once for several hours during a very severe winter, I cannot recommend this as a torrid amusement—indeed, the melancholy "sough" of the sea, and the pale glitter of the stars in the half-frozen pools, whose dead and dry sedges rustle in unison to the icy blasts rushing from the dead white north, make even the most hardy long for the old armchair by the cozy fireside.

A writer in the *Zoologist* some years ago appeared to think that iodine was a species of enchanter's wand in rendering your presence unknown to wildfowl. I have never tried it, having but little faith in cunning nostrums concocted for the taking of either birds or fish; but as he is a gentleman of standing and great experience, I will quote his words from which I drew my inference:

A cormorant once perched himself on my back as I lay concealed on a rock enveloped in a drab driving coat, which so closely resembled the rock in colour that even he was deceived, and, taking my back as the highest pinnacle, accommodated himself accordingly; neither did he discover his error till my hand grasped him by the legs. I have frequently had cormorants and shags perched around me within a few feet; but their suspicions seemed generally to be aroused by human smell, unless I had rubbed iodine on some part of my clothes.

The landrail or corncrake, whose peculiar rasping cry we hear in the grass or young corn in the spring of the year, is easily called to the gun by rubbing one notched bone over another, or, better still, using that peculiar instrument of torture worked at fairs, and called a "scratchback"—the same which, in the palmy days of Greenwich or Charlton fairs, was retailed to the cry of "All the fun of the fair for one penny!"

In bringing this chapter to a close, let me not omit to mention that all shot birds should immediately have the mouth, palatal slit, and nostrils, stopped with tow or cotton wool, to prevent the blood from running out and soiling the feathers; then, if possible, always wrap each specimen separately in paper, smoothing the feathers in their proper places before doing so. Also, never carry a shot bird by its neck, as the weight of the bird's body depending from the neck must stretch the latter beyond its fair proportions.

I have here briefly glanced at a few of the many ways of taking birds and beasts; to have described them all would have required a special volume double the size of the present one. I think, however, I have said enough for all practical needs; but in case any reader should require fuller information, I must refer him to such articles as he will find week by week in *The Field, Land and Water*, or the American publication, *Forest and Stream*. Good text books, also, on Trapping, &c., are W. B. Lord's "Shifts and Expedients of Camp Life," Captain Darwin's ("High Elms") "Game Preservers' Manual," Jefferries' "Amateur Poacher," "Gamekeeper at Home," &c. For details as to the hunting and scientific shooting of foreign large game, with directions as to the vulnerable spots to be aimed at, I must again refer the reader to articles from the pen of such men as Sir Samuel Baker, G. P. Sanderson, "Smoothbore," "The Old Shekarry," Gordon Cumming, Jules Gérard, C. J. Andersson, Emil Holub, F. C. Selous, &c., all of whom have either written books on sporting, or whose articles are still to be met with in late numbers of *The Field*.

LARK MIRRORS.

INQUIRIES are often made by those who care more for their seeds than for the birds that devour them, as to the best means of getting rid of Larks, which during the late autumn and winter months assemble in large flocks upon the cultivated lands, and occasion much trouble and loss to the farmers. " Getting rid of them " of course means catching or killing them; for to attempt to frighten them away would be a hopeless undertaking. The sentiment which at one time would have evoked an outburst of indignation at the notion of killing Larks seems to be gradually evaporating as people are getting to know more of the habits of birds from more attentive observation of their movements.

It was at one time supposed (perhaps many still believe it) that the Skylark is resident in the British Islands throughout the year, and that to destroy it by hundreds when congregated in flocks during the winter would surely deprive us in summer of the notes of one of our sweetest songsters. The published observations of modern naturalists, however, have shown this to be a fallacy; and it is now well ascertained that the Skylark is truly migratory in its habits, and that hundreds and thousands of these birds come over to this country from the Continent between the months of August and January.

It is perhaps not generally known that during the past three years, under the auspices of the British Association, systematic measures have been adopted by a committee of ornithologists, with a view of ascertaining the precise conditions of time, place, and weather under which the so-called migratory birds reach our shores at their respective seasons. This is sought to be achieved by enlisting the services of the keepers of lighthouses and light-ships on various parts of the coast, and getting them to record their observations on forms supplied to them for the purpose, from which at the end of each year tabulated results are worked out.

Turning to the last published report of this com-mittee,* we find numerous observations on the Sky-lark. Thus at page 42 :

Entries of the migration of the Skylark at the east-coast stations are far too numerous to note separately. In many cases they occupy a large portion of the returned schedules, and in-dividually far outnumber any other species. On our east coast they are noticed at thirty-one of the stations making returns, from the Farne Islands to the Casquets, Alderney.

Then follow details showing that at certain light-houses and lightships, on certain days during the months of September, October, and November, Skylarks were observed to arrive on the east coast in "numbers," "great numbers," "flocks," and "numerous flocks." Thus, at Spurn Lighthouse

* Report on the Migration of Birds in the Spring and Autumn of 1880. By J. A. Harvie Brown, J. Cordeaux, and P. Kermode. 8vo., pp. 120. Published by Sonnenschein and Co., 15, Pater-noster-square.

the arrival of flocks in October was "from the 9th to 15th, every day continuous." At Lynn Well light vessel, Oct. 11, 12, and 13, "continuous arrivals during day." At the Leman and Ower light vessel on eleven days in October, "day and night." At the Galloper light vessel, on seventeen days during October and November, "in large flocks up to five hundred in a flock." At four stations on the Goodwin Sands "enormous numbers crossed."   ·

This migration of the Skylark, says the reporter (Mr. Cordeaux), was carried on at all hours of the day and night, in all weathers, from Aug. 27th to Jan. 12th. The "great rush" took place during the last fortnight in October, more crossing probably on the 22nd than on any other day; and at Heligoland on the 20th and 21st. A second "rush" a month later, on or about Nov. 21st; and a third "rush" on the outbreak of severe weather in the second week in January, 1881. General line of direction E. to W., sometimes N.E. to S.W., but generally with a strong trend from points south of east. It is remarkable, as shown by the returns, how frequently Larks are associated in migration with Starlings, either in separate flocks or together; in fact, the two species seem to be inseparable. In a large majority of instances these two meadow-feeders are associated as if impelled to migrate by a common cause.

These observations suffice to set at rest the question whether Larks are migratory, and at the same time remove the objection which has been raised to their being killed here in numbers during the winter months. Then comes the question, if they may be killed, or (as some agriculturists would say) must be killed, how is this to be accomplished? Obviously either by netting or shooting. In days of yore, before the use of small shot was introduced, "the art of fowling" was a necessary part of the education of an English country gentleman; and

Larks, like game and wildfowl, were then taken abundantly in nets. Now the art is almost forgotten, and few probably know how to make and use a Lark net, except the professional bird-catchers, who derive a profit from the practice.

But, although the use of nets and lime-twigs has been almost entirely superseded by the use of guns, Lark-shooting in England is not regarded with much favour by the majority of shooters, being generally considered to be *infra dig.*, not worth the powder and shot, and so forth. In France, however, the case is far different. Not only are immense numbers of Larks taken there for the market by means of the night net, which the French call *traîneau*, but sportsmen in various parts of France shoot hundreds of these birds at the proper season by means of that ingenious contrivance called a "Lark mirror." The device is a very old one ; according to French authors as old as the time of Louis XIII. (1610), who first introduced in France the art of shooting flying. It is referred to by Shakespeare, and after him by various writers of the seventeenth century, but it has been supposed to be no older in origin than the date of the invention of small shot, which came into use in England in 1548.

It is most probable, however, that the Lark Mirror was originally the device of a fowler, and was used with a net some time before it came to be employed with a gun. This assumption at least seems warranted by the allusions made to its use by writers of the early part of the 17th century, who do not refer to it as a novel device, or as one then lately introduced. Thus, in "The Jewell for Gentrie," 1614, we read:—

There is another Stale belonging to these Day-nets, which is very proper and excellent, chiefly at the latter end of the yeere when Birds are least apt to play; and that is a three square piece of wood, a foote in length, and three inches each square; it must be painted red, and be all inlaid with square or round pieces of looking-glasse, it must have a foote in the midst, which must goe into a wide socket of wood, made in a strong stake, which must be stricken into the earth, then to the foote must be fastened a packthread, which being wounde many times about the foote, and issuing through a little hole of the stake, must come to your feete, so that when you pull it, the wood will turne so round, that it will give a strange reflection and so continuing the turning it will entice the Birds to play wonderfully; the place where you shall set it shall be by the stale, your Larke, so that you may use one string after another.

Markham certainly refers to the use of the mirror with nets. In his now scarce little volume, entitled "Hunger's Prevention, or the Art of Fowling," printed in 1621, he says (p. 116): "There is also another stale or inticement for these byrdes which is called the looking-glasse." This he describes at some length, and then proceeds: "Now both this and the other stale before spoken of [a live decoy bird] are to be placed in the very midst or centre betweene the two nets, and about two or three foote one distant from another, so that in the falling of the nets the cords may by no means touch or annoy them; neither must they stand one before or after another, but in a direct line one over against the other, the glasse being kept continually moving, and the bird very oft flickering."

When did the birdcatchers cease to employ this device with their nets? Apparently not for some considerable time after the introduction of shooting flying, and the employment of the mirror for lark shooting. Nicholas Cox, in his "Gentlemen's Recreation," 1674, referring to the capture of Larks, says "The next way of taking them is with a day net, and a glass, which is incomparable pastime on a frosty morning. These nets are commonly seven foot deep and fifteen long, knit with your French mesh and a very fine thread."

In a curious little book entitled "The Field Songster, or Bird Fancier's Delight" (1753), the author, whose name does not appear on the title, says (p. 31), "To take the Skylark in Flight.—You take them as you do other small birds—with a clap-net; in the country about Dunstable and several other places they take them with a glass called a larking-glass. These glasses are made of the bigness and shape of a cucumber, hollow within, and three, four, or five holes cut round, and pieces of looking glass placed in; it is fixed by a staff, and runs out like a whirligig, having a line which comes where we stand, at a pull-pin. We work it backwards and forwards. This must be of a sunshiny day, then the larks will play the better, the glass glittering and the larks playing about, and seeing themselves in it, makes them come down to it. As soon as they come within reach, pull the nets over them. By this I have known, in the country, ten or fifteen dozen taken in a morning."

But whatever the antiquity of Lark-mirrors may be, the contrivance is as efficacious as it is simple. There are various patterns in use at the present day in France, but all are constructed on the same principle. The simplest is a wooden spindle with a mushroom-shaped head, which is studded with small pieces of looking-glass set at various angles. Round the shank of the head which revolves upon the spindle, a long light line is wound, which, being carried some five and twenty yards by the shooter, is pulled by him in such a manner that the impetus gained by unwinding it causes the line to at once

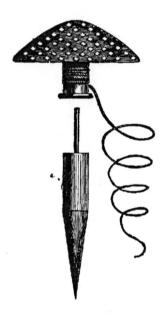

re-wind itself round the shank, and thus the glass is kept twirling as long as the shooter pleases. Some fasten the end of the line to one leg, which is kept in motion at the critical time when both hands are required for the gun ; others, to save trouble, employ a lad to pull the line for them. The remarkable feature about this device is the extraordinary fascination which the revolving and shining glass seems to exercise upon the unfortunate Larks.

They see it at a considerable distance, are attracted towards it, and positively hover over it (*faisant le Saint Esprit,* as French sportsmen call it), presenting the easiest possible mark for a charge of snipe shot.

All sorts of theories have been propounded to account for this singular fascination. Some (like Buffon) assert that the lark mistakes the shining

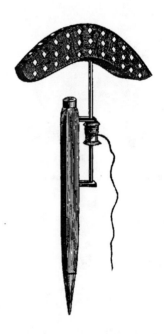

glass for running water; but, unfortunately for this theory, larks are not in any sense water-birds, and are more often met with on stubbles, fallows, and, generally speaking, dry situations. Another pretty theory is that the small facets of the mirror sparkling in the autumn sun so much resemble dew-drops, that the migrating birds are deluded into fancying that summer has come again, and with it all that is most grateful to a lark's palate, in that shining spot which seems to offer attractions for food and rest after their long flight. A third notion is that the bird, so fond of soaring to enjoy the warm rays of a summer sun, mistakes the mirror for the sun; and only discovers its error when meeting with a warm reception of a very different kind, namely, that which ardent sportsmen delight to extend to everything with feathers that comes within their range.

In the absence of any certain knowledge on the subject, it seems most reasonable to suppose that *curiosity* is really the motive which impels the bird to its fate. Curiosity we know impels the fowl upon a decoy pond to enter the pipe and follow the decoy-man's little dog which gradually lures them to destruction. Curiosity, too, has induced many a wild animal to come within range of the hunter's rifle when the owner, lying prostrate and concealed, has slowly waved a small red flag upon a wand affixed to his boot. Curiosity, then, in all probability, attracts the lark to the mirror.

Vast numbers, as stated, are in this way allured and shot. The conditions considered most favourable for this sport by our French neighbours are a fine October morning, with a slight frost and the wind in the east. In addition to this, a good deal will depend upon the position taken up by the shooter; for it is not enough to possess a mirror and be a tolerably good shot. One must take up one's position, so to say, in the very wake of the migrating flocks, and to be on the right or left of the line of their direction means comparatively little shooting.

As the wildfowl-shooter observes the line taken by the ducks at flight time, so the lark-shooter must note the direction in which his smaller quarry is migrating, and, availing himself of a certain amount of concealment (as, for instance, in a hollow or behind a bush), must study both sun and wind. It is needless to say he must not face the sun; nor is it advisable that it should be entirely at his back. The best light is a side light, the mirror being set up in such a position that a few feet of horizon may be seen clearly above it. Care should be taken also, when fixing the spindle in the ground, to make the mirror lean slightly away from the gun, so as to prevent its catching and checking the line when pulled. It is important also to see that the ground is sufficiently clear along the course of the line; it would never do, for instance, to lay it in high stubble.

With regard to the wind; when it is in the north, the Larks fly fast and seem loth to stop. With a southerly wind they fly low, and often hang about without taking much notice of the mirror. Should it blow from W.S.W. the passage is often considerable, but this wind is almost always accompanied with a cloudy sky, in which case the mirror is not seen well at a distance, and becomes practically almost useless. An east wind is the best of all, for that usually brings plenty of Larks, travelling leisurely, and stopping more readily to hover around the mirror.

The shooter should be on the ground about half-past seven or eight, and stay till about eleven or twelve, at which time the tide of migration seems to ebb, and the birds alight to rest and feed. In the north and east of France Lark shooting with mirrors (*la chasse d'alouettes au miroir*) is generally carried on between Oct. 1 and Nov. 10; in the south somewhat later.

An old hand at this sport, on being asked whether smoking was permissible while lying in wait, or whether it would deter the Larks from approaching, replied with a grin, " Mais oui; fumez tant qu'il vous plaira, *mais* ayez soin de ne fumer que du bon tabac; car l'odeur du tabac inférieur (du tabac Allemand, par exemple) est désagréable à l'allouette!" What reply would a German lark shooter have made to the same question?

I ascertained when last in Paris that Lark Mirrors may be obtained there of Rédillard, 25, Rue Notre Dame de Nazareth, and in London they used to be made by Bellchambers of 221, Waterloo Road.

PLOVER CATCHING IN FRANCE.

La Chasse aux Pluviers in many parts of France is quite an institution, and the time and trouble which is expended at the proper season to secure these *bonnes-bouches* may 'well be thought worthy of a nobler quarry. Guns, snares, nets, bird-calls, and call-birds, are in turn brought into requisition, and the leader of a flock or " wing " must indeed be a crafty bird if he can save his companions from the destruction which threatens them on all sides.

The Golden Plover in France is only a migratory species, passing through the country twice a year, in spring and autumn, and does not, as in England, remain to nest. It is therefore only for a short time at these seasons that the *chasseurs* can carry on their sport. The months of March and September are said to be the most favourable for Plover catching. In March the birds are on their way northward for the nesting season. In September they are moving southward with their young for the winter. Larger numbers, as a rule, are taken in the latter month; for the flocks then consist for the most part of young birds, which, being less suspicious in their nature, are more readily ensnared.

Of the various methods employed for their

capture, there is no doubt that the net is the most destructive; and it has this advantage over the gun, that the birds when caught are sent to market without loss of blood and feathers, which disfigures their appearance and lessens their weight.

The most favourable time for netting is said to be at early dawn, when the flocks begin to answer the call of their leader—the *sentinelle* or *Pluvier appellant*, as the French call it. A long net or *rideau de filet* is stretched across the ground, facing a spot where the birds have been observed to roost the night before. The *chasseurs* then surround the flock, and, advancing in line, put them up, and with much shouting and throwing of sticks drive them towards the net, into which they fly pell-mell. The net falls, and numbers are entangled in the meshes. It sometimes happens that an entire flock is taken in this way.

If a birdcatcher, or *oiseleur*, goes to work single-handed, he manages somewhat differently. He conceals himself behind the net, and calls the birds towards it, instead of driving them into it. Many bird-catchers can imitate the call of a Plover so well with their lips that they have no need to use a regular bird-call (*appeau*). Those, however, who are not so gifted, avail themselves of a very ingenious contrivance to answer the purpose. The leg bone of a goat is sawn to the length of about three inches, and cut transversely at both ends, one end of which is stopped with wax. Three round holes are then bored in the tube, one near the closed end to whistle on, a second just below it, in which a quill is inserted, and a third at the other end, larger than the other two, and closer to the sides of the bone. With this instrument they do wonders, imitating the Plover's note to perfection, and, as occasion requires, giving all the modulations which render their wild and melancholy cry so pleasing to the ear.

The decoy-birds used are termed *appelans* or *entes*, according as they are alive or stuffed. In the former case peewits are always used, not only because they are birds of similar habits to the Golden Plover, consorting with them in a state of nature, and acting the part of sentinels, but also because they are easily tamed, and will feed readily in confinement. They are pegged down with short lines, giving them just enough play to enable them to move about in a small circle, and rise a foot or so off the ground when pulled by a check-string. The Plovers, seeing their wary friends the Peewits apparently at their ease, answer the birdcatcher's call, and fly towards them. They are then either taken gradually by the nooses into which they walk, or are put up and shot as soon as they come within range.

The device employed with what the French call *entes* has long been known in England amongst our fen-men, and is still practised on a small scale by the men who are employed to catch Linnets, Goldfinches, and Chaffinches for the trade. The old English equivalent for the French term is "stale." It· is simply a stuffed bird of the species which the fowler wishes to decoy, set up in as natural a position as possible, either before a net or in the midst of several springes. Imitating the call of the passing birds, the fowler attracts their attention to to the "stale" or "stales," and, as soon as they alight, they are either caught in the snares or the net is pulled over them.

Beaumont and Fletcher speak of "stales to catch kites" (Hum. Lieut., iii., 2). Sometimes a live bird is pegged down as soon as caught instead of a stuffed one, and is doubtless much more effective; for, as Sidney says ("Arcadia, ii., p. 169), "One bird caught serves as a 'stale' to bring in more." Shakespeare, as I have pointed out elsewhere,* has employed the word "stale" in this sense in the "Comedy of Errors" (Act ii., sc. 1), "The Tempest" (Act iv., sc. 1), and "The Taming of the Shrew" (Act iii., sc. 1). At page 18 of "The Experienced Fowler," a curious little volume, published in 1704, the reader is thus instructed, "How to make a Stale": "You may shoot a Lark or some other bird; take out the entrails, stuff him with tow, and dry him in an oven, his wings set in a flying posture; and so you may be furnished at all times." This device was chiefly resorted to formerly for taking the Ruff and Reeve, and other fen birds, which fetched good prices for the table.

A mode of killing Plovers by night has been adopted with more or less success by French *chasseurs*. It is well known that many birds which fly by night are powerfully attracted by a bright light, and, taking advantage of this, the fowlers go out in a party at night, one of them carrying a large lantern on a pole. They use their bird-calls until they hear them replied to, then advance in line, the light being

* "The Ornithology of Shakespeare," p. 245.

carried on the side nearest to the birds. The latter come dashing along with wild cries, sweep over or past the light, and are "cut into" by the whole party as they go by,

In the matter of bird-calls the French may be allowed to excel us, and amongst many of their ingenious inventions in this line they contrive a very effective and simple call for the Peewit. They take a piece of wood about three inches long, and somewhat thicker than the little finger, split it half-way down, and insert in the slit a piece of ivy or laurel leaf. With this in their mouth they can so beguile a Plover that they have only to hold up the net and— *le voilà.*

When bringing the gun into operation by day, they avail themselves at the same time of both bird-calls and call-birds. The latter are pegged down in position; the sportsmen, pushing a screen of twigs before them, advance slowly, and put up the Plovers. The live call-birds, seeing them on the wing, try and rise too; but, "the mountain being unable to come to Mahomet," Mahomet (with all his tribe) obligingly comes to the mountain, and pays the penalty. A fusillade is opened from the little screens, and dead and dying quickly strew the ground.

But is this sport? Surely it is taking "a mean advantage." No! Leave screens and call-birds behind. Seek the Plovers in their wild haunts if you *will;* stalk them if you *can;* and *then,* if the powder be "straight," and you fill your pockets, tramp merrily home, and talk of Sport.